RECORDER

GRADES 3–4

SPOTLIGHT on MUSIC™

SERIES AUTHORS

Judy Bond	Michael Jothen
René Boyer	Chris Judah-Lauder
Margaret Campbelle-Holman	Carol King
Emily Crocker	Vincent P. Lawrence
Marilyn C. Davidson	Ellen McCullough-Brabson
Robert de Frece	Janet McMillion
Virginia Ebinger	Nancy L.T. Miller
Mary Goetze	Ivy Rawlins
Betsy M. Henderson	Susan Snyder
John Jacobson	Gilberto D. Soto

Kodály Contributing Consultant
Sr. Lorna Zemke

Mc Graw Hill Macmillan McGraw-Hill

ACKNOWLEDGMENTS

Grateful acknowledgment is given to the following authors, composers, and publishers. Every effort has been made to trace the ownership of all copyrighted material and to secure the necessary permissions to reprint these selections. In the case of some selections for which acknowledgment is not given, extensive research has failed to locate the copyright holders.

Writer
Virginia Ebinger

Macmillan/McGraw-Hill School Division
2 Penn Plaza
New York, New York 10121

Printed in the United States of America
ISBN: 0-02-295824-X
4 5 6 7 8 9 024 06 05

Introduction

Spotlight on Music: Recorder contains soprano recorder activities for Macmillan/ McGraw-Hill's SPOTLIGHT ON MUSIC series, Grades 3 and 4. The activities are on reproducible black-line masters that can be duplicated and distributed to each student. Some teachers may wish to create overhead transparencies to use in addition to, or in place of, individual copies for each student. Teaching suggestions are on the back of each black-line master for easy reference and use during the recorder lesson.

The first half of the book, Lessons 1–17, teaches beginning soprano recorder using pitches G A B E and is correlated to SPOTLIGHT ON MUSIC, Grade 3. The second half of the book, Lessons 18–36, begins with a review of the earlier pitches but moves more quickly, adding low and high D, high C, and F♯. It is correlated to SPOTLIGHT ON MUSIC, Grade 4. This makes it possible to use Lessons 1–17 for beginning Grade 3 students, and to start with Lesson 18 for beginning Grade 4 students.

Most recorder lessons include songs from the Student Book lesson referred to on the Recorder Master page. Activities requiring different levels of skills are included to accommodate the needs of all the students. Playalongs with SPOTLIGHT ON MUSIC recordings give students the opportunity to experience the fun and challenges of ensemble playing right from the beginning.

This resource contains the following:

- Fingering charts (on black-line masters and on the last page).

- Practice patterns, teaching suggestions, and tips on recorder technique.

- Play-alongs, descants, harmony parts, ostinatos, and simple melodies.

- Opportunities for student improvisation and composition.

- Creative activities related to songs in the black-line masters.

We are sure that this resource will be a valuable addition to your overall music program. Along with reinforcing note-reading and basic music theory, recorder can be an integral part of the Orff process. In addition, recorder playing provides students with an excellent foundation for participation in your school's instrumental music program.

Table of Contents

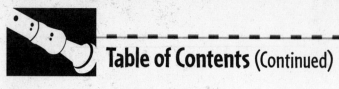

Table of Contents (Continued)

Name _____ Date _____

Beginning with B

Let's begin to play the recorder—and there's no better way to begin than with B!

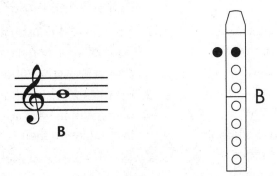

Three things you need to pay attention to as you learn to play the recorder are:

1. Your breath

2. Your fingers

3. Your ears

Pick up your recorder with your left hand. Hold it as you held your "arm recorder." Your left thumb covers the hole on the back, and your left pointer finger covers the top hole on the front. Support it lightly with your right hand. Now sit tall, and hold your recorder straight down in front of you.

Place the mouthpiece of your recorder on your lower lip, and then close your upper lip around it. Don't touch your teeth.

Watch and listen as your teacher plays "Hot Cross Buns."

• Clap the rhythm.

• Whisper "doo" in the correct rhythm into the recorder.

Hot Cross Buns

Now you know B! You'll learn many other notes on your recorder, but for now B is enough!

Pitch: B

Objectives

- Students will learn the proper techniques for holding and playing the recorder.
- Students will learn to play B on the recorder.

Preparation

- Discuss the basic principles of learning to play any instrument: start slowly and carefully, and learn basic techniques correctly to avoid problems later on.
- Introduce the "arm recorder." Have students put their right arms in the air and make their right hands into fists. Have them place their right fists under their chins, elbows down. The right wrists have become "arm recorders" and are helpful for teaching proper technique.
- Explain how to finger B on the "arm recorder."
- Have students place their thumbs on the pulse at the back of their wrists and then place their index fingers opposite their thumbs on the front of their wrists.
- Next have students feel their finger pads, the flat, fleshy parts of their fingers. This part of the fingers covers the holes of the recorder. It is very important that these holes be completely covered.

Procedure

- Have students pick up recorders with their left hands and hold them in the position of their "arm recorders," placing their right hands at the bottom of the recorders.
- Have students practice holding the recorder mouthpiece on the chin, with left hand thumb and fingers in the proper position, when listening to instructions or waiting to play.
- Guide students through the activities of R•1.

- Explain the three most important things to pay attention to when learning the recorder.
  1. Breath—Explain that when students put the recorder's mouthpiece between their lips, they must breathe very gently into it as they whisper "doo."
  2. Fingers—Demonstrate how to place the pads of your fingers straight across the proper holes, covering them completely.
  3. Ears—Emphasize that students must always listen very carefully to the sounds they make on their recorders.
- Review the basics of recorder technique.
  1. Place the mouthpiece between the lips, not between the teeth. Place it on the lower lip, and then close the upper lip over it.
  2. Keep the left hand at the top, and cover the holes completely with pads of the fingers.
  3. Breathe very gently into the recorder when playing.
  4. Tonguing should be a whispered "doo" on each note.
- Play the melody for "Hot Cross Buns," and then play the descant. Have students clap the rhythm of the descant and then whisper "doo" to the rhythm. Finally, have students whisper "doo" into the recorder, using the rhythm of the descant.
- Play the melody for "Hot Cross Buns" while the students play the descant in rhythm.
- For additional practice, have students work with partners and take turns echoing each other as they play B in different rhythms.
- Organize students into groups of six or eight. Invite them to take turns singing and playing. One student should play the descant while the others in the group sing "Hot Cross Buns."

Name _____ Date _____

Playing with B

Think about what you have learned.

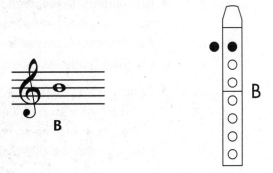

B

Now let's practice.

- Sit tall.
- Place your left thumb over the back hole and your pointer finger over the top hole.
- Support the bottom of the recorder with your right hand.
- Place the mouthpiece on your lower lip, and then close your upper lip over it.
- Echo what your teacher plays. First sing the pitch name, and then play it.

Sing "Tanabata" with the recording. The song is on page 62 of your book.

- Clap the rhythm of the recorder pattern.
- Play the recorder pattern on B.
- Play the pattern with the song.

Tanabata

Play the first four measures 3 times

Pitch: B

Using Recorder Master R•2

Objectives

- Students will review playing B.

- Students will learn a playalong for "Tanabata."

Preparation

- Have students review fingering B: Place mouthpiece on chin, just under the lower lip. Place left thumb on the back of the recorder and the index finger over the proper holes, with the right hand lightly supporting the recorder. (This prepares the correct position, ready for playing.)

- Play various rhythm patterns and have students play B, echoing the patterns you play.

- Teach students the three-part echo plan:

  1. Listen and finger notes.

  2. Sing pitch names and finger notes.

  3. Play.

Procedure

- Ask students to tell what they now know about playing the recorder (how to hold the instrument, proper tonguing ("doo"), covering the holes, posture, breathing).

- Review "Hot Cross Buns." Clap the rhythm of the playalong, and then play it. Have half of the class sing the song while the other half performs the playalong. Switch parts.

- Have students review "Tanabata" (page 62), singing it and listening to the recording. Discuss its quiet mood, and relate that to playing the recorder quietly to accompany it.

- Clap the rhythm of the playalong. Discuss the change of the pattern in the last measure.

- Have students sing the rhythm on B with the recorder in place on the chin.

- Have students play the playalong first without the song, and then with it.

Name _____ Date _____

Advancing to A

B is a very nice note, but we can't stay on it forever.

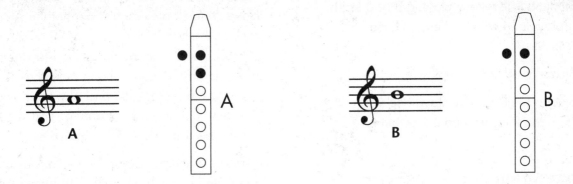

What are the three important things about playing the recorder? Let's add a fourth: eyes. Your eyes let you see that B sits in the middle of the staff on a line. A is just below it in a space.

Let's learn how to play A. Still covering the front and back holes for B, put your middle finger down to cover the next hole. Breathe gently into the recorder, whispering "doo."

Sing "Golden Ring Around the Susan Girl" on page 264 in your book. Clap the rhythm below as you listen to the recording. Clap and sing A, and then play it.

Golden Ring Around the Susan Girl

Pitches: B A

Using Recorder Master R•3

Objectives

- Students will review playing B and learn a playalong with "Butterfly, Come Play with Me."
- Students will learn to play A.
- Students will learn a playalong with "Golden Ring Around the Susan Girl."

Preparation

- Have students review rules for breathing, posture, playing position, and fingering for B.
- Using three-part echo form (listen, sing, play), have students echo teacher, playing B on various short rhythm patterns.
- Have two or three students take turns being teacher, giving patterns to echo on B.

Procedure

- Ask students to answer the question at the beginning of R•3. (breath, fingers, ears)
- Discuss the difference between line notes and space notes: When a line runs through a note, it is on a line; a space note is in a space between two lines.

- Guide students through a playalong with "Butterfly, Come Play with Me" (page 112). Have them clap every first beat of the A section, both times it occurs, as they listen to the recording, and then play the first beats on B. (It may be confusing to them that A signifies the first section and also the name of a new note they are learning. You should clarify this if it seems to be a problem.)
- Perform "Butterfly, Come Play with Me" as suggested in the book, with Orff instruments accompanying the B section, but now with the added attraction of the recorders playing in the A sections.
- Have students find fingering for A. Have them practice covering both holes simultaneously. Remind students of the three-part echo (finger, sing the letter name, play). Play some short rhythm patterns on A for them to echo.
- Lead them through the steps to learn the playalong for "Golden Ring Around the Susan Girl" (page 264). Have half the class play the recorder part while the other half sings the song. Then switch roles.

Name _____ Date _____

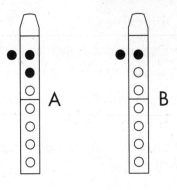

Time for Two Notes

You can play B, and you can play A. Remember that
B is the line note in the middle of the staff. A sits right
below it in a space between the lines.

A

B

Play along with the recording of "Coral" on page 249 in your book.
Clap the rhythm first. Words that fit the rhythm will help you: *Oh white
coral*. Sing that rhythm on A as you listen to the recording. Then play it
on your recorder.

Coral

Oh   white cor-al

Sing and play echoes to the notes your teacher plays. Be sure to listen
carefully. Think which note sounds higher than the other—that would be B.

Now play along with "Bella Bimba."

Bella Bimba

Pitches: B A

Using Recorder Master R•4

Objectives

- Students will review A and learn a playalong with "Coral."

- Students will distinguish between A and B in echo phrases.

- Students will learn a playalong with "Bella Bimba."

Preparation

- Review the three-part echo pattern to reinforce it with students (listen and finger, sing pitch names and finger, play). The echo pattern becomes more and more important as more notes are learned.

- Have volunteers demonstrate proper posture, breathing, tonguing (whispered "doo"), and fingering.

- Review fingering for B and A. Have students respond to echoes on each of the two notes with varied rhythm patterns, especially stressing patterns in triple meter.

Procedure

- Have students describe the difference between A and B as they appear on the staff.

- Introduce the playalong for "Coral" (page 249). Have students learn the rhythm by reading and speaking and then clapping words: "Oh white coral" | ♩ | ♩ ♫ |. Then have students play along with the recording.

- When students are able to respond correctly to echoes on A and on B, make short combinations of the two notes for them to echo. (It is easier for them to go from B to A than from A to B.)

- Have each student work with a partner, taking turns giving and receiving A and B echoes.

- Lead students in the playalong to "Bella Bimba" (page 172). Have students identify places where A occurs. Then pat, clap, and snap the rhythm to illustrate triple meter.

- Have students sing the pitches of the playalong with the recording and then play them on the recorder.

Name _____ Date _____

Practice Makes Perfect

"Chicka-ma, Chicka-ma, Craney Crow" on page 263 in your book will be an easy playalong for you. It's all on B. Clap and speak the rhythm first: *crow, crow, chicka-ma crow.*

Chicka-ma, Chicka-ma, Craney Crow

Another playalong using only B is "The Paw Paw Patch" on page 195 in your book. Words that fit the rhythm will help you. For what rhythm could you use *dear little Nell?* For what rhythm could you use *paw paw patch?*

The Paw Paw Patch

Follow your teacher's directions for singing and playing "Shalom Chaveyrim" on page 141 in your book.

Shalom Chaveyrim

Pitch: B

Using Recorder Master R•5

Objective

- Students will gain competency in playing B.

Preparation

- Begin the lesson with practice in echoing the notes the students have learned so far: A and B.

- Have the students create a "Recorder Wave." Have students stand side-by-side in a line or circle. Have one person begin playing. Each following person begins playing when he or she hears the person before him/her begin playing and stop when he or she hears the person after him or her begin to play. Perform the Recorder Wave on B.

- But first, of course, remind students to sit tall, to breathe "doo" gently into their recorders, to hold it correctly and cover the holes completely, and to listen very, very carefully.

Procedure

- Have students sing "Chicka-ma, Chicka-ma, Craney Crow" (page 263) with or without the recording, establishing a feel for the rhythm. Then have them clap the recorder's rhythm before they play it.

- Organize the class into three groups so that some sing, some play recorder, and some dramatize the action. Switch parts so that everyone has an opportunity to participate in each activity. Let the recorders play an A for the count at the end of the verses.

- Practice the rhythm of "The Paw Paw Patch" (page 195) by patting on alternating legs, and then practice the rhythm of the playalong by clapping the quarter notes and patting the eighths and sixteenths.

- Sing "Shalom Chaveyrim" (page 141) in unison. Have students listen to the recording and very lightly clap the rhythm of the playalong. Remind them to listen carefully to their sound when they play with the recording. Organize the class into two groups. Have half of the class sing while the other half plays. Then switch roles.

Name _____   Date _____

Just Playing Around

- Today you get to take turns playing the echo-giver. Play a phrase on B or A for the class to echo. Your phrase can include all Bs, all As, or both Bs and As. Be careful not to make it too hard or too long—you might have to repeat it!

- Look at this playalong for "Circle Round the Zero." Be careful! There are some unexpected changes in the rhythm. Sometimes the rest comes before a B, and sometimes it comes after a B.

Circle Round the Zero

The next playalong is for the chorus of the song "Hey Motswala" on page 34 of your book. Before you play it, place your recorder on your chin in playing position. Then finger and sing the Bs and As in their proper rhythm.

Hey, Motswala (chorus only)
Descant on A and B

Let your introduction set the marching tempo for this playalong for "Charlie."

Charlie
Playalong on B and A

Pitches: B A

Using Recorder Master R•6

Objective

- Students will learn playalongs using B and A for "Circle Round the Zero," "Hey, Motswala," and "Charlie."

Preparation

- Check that students' posture is correct for playing, and remind them about breath control and proper holding of the instrument.

Procedure

- Make sure that the class follows the three-part echo plan: listen and finger the notes, sing pitches and finger the notes, and then play an echo of what they have heard.

- Allow several students a chance to play phrases with B and A for the class to echo. Suggest that the phrases be only four beats to begin with. As students gain confidence, they can play six- and eight-beat phrases.

- Direct students' attention to the rhythmic surprises in "Circle Round the Zero" (page 267). Demonstrate the descant as it is written. This will help students learn to play it correctly. Have students point out the rests that come before a B and the rests that come after a B. Ask students to clap and sing the As and Bs in the playalong as they listen to the recording. Finally, have students play the descant on their recorders.

- Have students practice patterns of pat, clap, snap to prepare them for triple meter in playing "Hey, Motswala" (page 34). Direct them to sing the verse, holding their recorders ready to play immediately after the upbeat on the chorus.

- Have one group of students play Orff instruments while another plays the playalong for "Charlie" (page 208). The percussionists should play the rhythm of the recorder part. When the recorders are playing B, percussionists should play E and B; when the recorders are playing A, the percussionists should play D and A.

Name _____ Date _____

Going On to G

Give yourself a hand! You're really learning to play the recorder. You might say it's in the BAG!

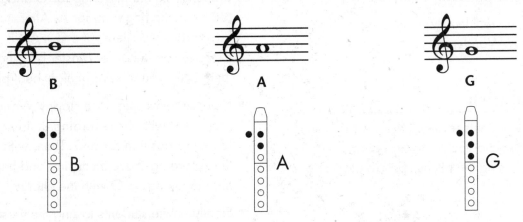

Now that you can play B and A, you will find G quite easy. Look at the picture that shows how to play G. Practice with the recorder on your chin, and then play the new note.

Place your recorder on your chin, and try these fingering exercises.

B – A   B – A – B   B – A – G
A – B   A – G   G – A – B

Sing the pitch names as you finger those notes, and then play them.

"The Happy Wanderer" is on page 18 in your book. Sing the verse, and play the descant on the chorus. It's a playalong on G.

The Happy Wanderer
Playalong on G

Pitches: G A B

Using Recorder Master R•7

Objectives

- Students will learn to play G.
- Students will learn a playalong to "The Happy Wanderer."

Preparation

- Have students review fingering for B and A and echo you on several phrases, being sure to sing the pitches before playing them.

Procedure

- Demonstrate the fingering for G and how it relates to the fingering for A. After students have practiced silently the G – A – B exercises on Recorder Master R•7, have them echo you in several eight-beat phrases.

- Have students sing "The Happy Wanderer" (page 18) with the recording, holding the fingering position for a G. Then, with the recording, have them sing and finger the playalong on G with the chorus.

- Finally, invite students to sing the verse and play the recorder part on the chorus.

Three Fingers Down

A finger and a thumb for B, add a finger for A, and three fingers down makes G!

Start off with echo-playing with a partner. Use short phrases. Concentrate on listening and then singing and fingering the correct pitches. That will make it easier to play them.

On page 278 in your book you will find "My Horses Ain't Hungry." While some of your classmates play the instrument part at the bottom of the page in your book, play the recorder playalong here.

My Horses Ain't Hungry
Playalong on G

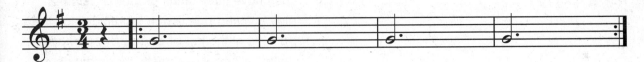

Listen to the recording of "Old Roger" on page 280 while you pat the beat. When you listen a second time, sing the pitches of the descant. Then play the descant.

Old Roger
Descant on G A B

Pitches: G A B

Using Recorder Master R•8

Objective

- Students will learn a playalong using G, A, and B.

Preparation

- Review fingering for B, A, and G. Have students practice moving between them, silently fingering and saying the pitches.

- Play phrases for echoing. Begin by telling students which note you will be starting on, and then have them figure it out. Pair students to practice additional echoes on B, A, and G.

Procedure

- Perform "My Horses Ain't Hungry" (page 278) as suggested. The class may be organized into thirds, each group having a turn at singing, playing melodic percussion, and playing recorder on the playalong. If you have an alto xylophone in your classroom, use it with the recorder because the two instruments complement each other's sounds. However, other instruments may also be used to play the melody.

- Have students work through suggestions for "Old Roger" on Recorder Master R•8. Then have three small groups of students play untuned percussion instruments on the patterns at the top of page 280, perhaps rhythm sticks or castanets, maracas, and guiro. A fourth group should perform the playalong on the recorder.

Name _____ Date _____

A Bag of Tunes

It should feel comfortable for you to use your three left-hand fingers now.

Every time you learn a new note, you can play more songs on your recorder. Look what you can do now that you know G as well as B and A.

Hot Cross Buns

You can also play the first part of "Frère Jacques." Begin on a G.

Here's another old French folk song, "Au clair de la lune," that asks you to perform a duet with yourself. Play the first part and repeat it. Sing the second part. Then play the first part again.

Au clair de la lune

Are there any other songs that you might be able to play with B, A, and G?

Pitches: G A B

Using Recorder Master R•9

Objective

- Students will to play tunes with B, A, G, both by reading and by ear.

Preparation

- Give students a few eight-beat phrases on G, A, B to echo, and then have them make up a new phrase of the same length. Let them all do this together a few times, and then ask for a volunteer to make up a phrase.

- Review with students the musical alphabet, reminding them that it goes only from A through G and then starts again at A.

Procedure

- Discuss the direction of the melody of "Hot Cross Buns," relating the visual downward movement on the staff to the downward sound of B, A, G. Show them that to go down on the staff is to go backward in the musical A through G alphabet.

- Guide students in exploring what they can play using only the pitches B, A, and G. Have them play a canon ("interrupted echo") on "Hot Cross Buns," with the second part starting on measure 3.

- Students can play "Frère Jacques" beginning on G. The pattern is G – A – B – G G – A – B – G.

- Have students read, sing, and finger the pitches of the A section of "Au clair de la lune" and then play it on their recorders. Read and sing the pitches of the B section, noting the downward sound and staff movement, as well as the backward alphabet.

- Encourage students to experiment to find other melodies that use only G, A, and B.

A Little Detective Work

There are three songs on this page. Each of them uses the same three notes—G, A, and B. There are other things about them that are the same, too. Can you discover what they are?

Night Song

German Lullaby

What's in Your Bag?

Virginia Nylander Ebinger

From G to B and Back Again

Virginia Nylander Ebinger

Pitches: G A B

Using Recorder Master R•10

Objective

- Students will identify similarities and differences among three G A B songs.

Preparation

- Begin of the class with echo work. Vary your phrase endings so that some end on G, giving a "home" sound, and others end on A or B, with a more unfinished sound.

Procedure

- Ask students to read and sing the pitch names while fingering the notes to "Night Song." Then have them play the song a couple of times to familiarize themselves with its tonality.

- Then have students read and sing pitch names while fingering the notes to "What's in Your Bag?" and then play the song two times.

- Finally, have students read and sing pitch names while fingering the notes to "From G to B and Back Again" and play the song two times.

- Ask students to identify the similarities and differences among the three pieces. (Similarities: Same notes: B, A, and G; all are in the key of G; all have same ending tone. Differences: Meter signatures; two are eight measures long, and one is ten measures long.)

- Discuss with students how ending on G gives a feeling of "home" or finality when only the three pitches are used.

Name _____ Date _____

Half and Half

So far you have learned three pitches—B, A, and G. You've played the pitches as a descant to a song and as the melody for a song. Now you will play a piece that is part descant and part melody. Can you figure out which part is melody and which part is descant?

Find "Woke Up This Morning" on pages 180 and 181 in your book, and then sing along with the recording. Clap the beat on the first section, and tap your heels on the second section (page 181).

Play the descant shown below on the first section. Tap your heels on the second section. Then repeat the descant when the first section returns.

Woke Up This Morning

Keep your breath flowing smoothly while you hold the longer notes.

Pitches: G A B

Using Recorder Master R•11

Objective

• Students will identify the descant and melody portions they are playing for "Woke Up This Morning."

Preparation

• Begin with echo practice. Be sure to include some long notes, and talk with students about holding the sound through long notes. Students should continue to breathe smoothly. Tell then never to push their breath.

Procedure

• Direct students to sing "Woke Up This Morning" (page 180) with the recording, clapping or patting the beat. Have students sing it again and follow the instructions on page 181 concerning whole note observance. (Tip: The heel taps come on the unaccented beats—2 and 4—of each measure.)

• Have students identify the places in the music where the melody of the song takes over from the descant.

• Point out that the commas above the staff indicate where students should take breaths.

• Have them play the refrain, "stayed on freedom" each of the three times it occurs and then play the last four and a half measures.

• Have students play the entire descant.

• Invite students to perform with recording. Some students might choose to play untuned percussion instruments for the rhythmic playalong on page 181.

Recorder Master R • 12

Afterthoughts and Fill-ins

"Over My Head" is an African American spiritual with long notes—some held for five beats—in the middle and at the end of three of its phrases. Follow your teacher's directions. Play this descant to the song with the recording, and then play it with half of the class singing the song.

Over My Head

Try this descant for "Sun Don't Set in the Mornin'."

Sun Don't Set in the Mornin'
Descant on A and B

Pitches: G A B

Using Recorder Master R•12

Objective

• Students will learn descants that occupy the time of long notes or a series of rests.

Preparation

• Play a game of Excuse Me for Interrupting. Have students echo-clap the simple rhythmic phrase shown below. The leader continues with these or other short rhythmic phrases as students interrupt with the same pattern. When they understand the plan, have them play their phrase on B as the leader plays his or her phrase on G.

Procedure

• Ask students to sing "Over My Head" (page 286) with the recording, at first patting the beat throughout and then patting only the whole notes tied to the quarters.

• Explain the tie as an extension of sound.

• Read and finger the descant on the recorder without the melody, but making sure that the parts occur at the correct time in the beat pattern.

• Have half of the class sing as the other half plays the descant, and then switch parts.

• Ask students to sing "Sun Don't Set in the Mornin'" (page 48) with the recording. Discuss the places where the descant "interrupts" or fills in rests. The descant is played only in the A section.

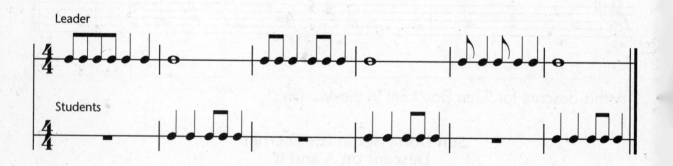

Name _____   Date _____

You Know the Answer

The thing a question needs most is—an answer! In this lesson, we're going to answer many questions, but not in words. Our questions and answers will be musical.

Look at these questions and answers.

Q: Where you going?   **Q:** What is the book about?

A: I'm going to town.   **A:** The book is about dogs.

A good answer is about as long as the question it answers. It also has part of the question in it, and it comes to a convincing end. You can see that in the questions and answers above.

The same is true in musical questions and answers. Here are some samples.

Play questions and answers with a partner. One of you can play the question, and the other can play the answer. Begin with these examples, and then make up some of your own.

Pitches: G A B

Using Recorder Master R • 13

Objective

- Students will create musical questions and answers.

Preparation

- Review B, A, G and students' ability to recognize and repeat them. Play short phrases and have students listen with their eyes closed and echo what you played.

Procedure

- Discuss all kinds of questions and answers: words, rhythmic, melodic. Remind students what makes a good answer to a question.

- Clap short rhythmic phrases for students first to echo and then to answer with a complementary phrase rather than an exact echo. You may want to model this procedure by having a student volunteer clap a question while you answer with a complementary rhythmic phase.

- Play short melodic patterns for the whole class to respond to, at first in exact echoes and then in complementary, answering phrases. Point out that questions often sound "unfinished," and answers have a finished sound to them, ending the musical phrase.

- Guide them through the question/answer activities on their Recorder Master.

Name _____ Date _____

Going Your Way

This lesson features you and a partner as the composers of a song.

Here are the words for your song.

> Apple tree, apple tree,
> Will your apple fall on me?
> I won't cry and I won't shout
> If your apple knocks me out.

Here are some suggestions to help you and your partner create your composition:

- Read the words several times silently, and then read them aloud.

- Think about the rhythm of the words, and then clap them.

- Remember how you worked with questions and answers in the last lesson.

- Using B, A, and G, experiment with a tune one phrase at a time.

- Play the notes in any order, using a rhythm you choose. The ending should be on G.

- When you figure out how you want your song to sound, practice it so that you will remember it.

- Perform the song with your partner for the class.

Pitches: G A B

Using Recorder Master R•14

Objective

• Students will compose music for a poem.

Preparation

• Remind students of how their question/ answer phrases worked. Have them echo a few phrases and then improvise phrases that are complements to those you play for them.

Procedure

• Read the poem aloud with your students. Emphasize the poem's rhythmic pattern (see below).

• Guide students through the suggested steps on their Recorder Master.

• Invite students to share their compositions with the class.

Round and Round and Back Again

In this lesson, you get to be a composer again and create a rondo. A rondo is a musical form that is fun, but it is also very easy. Even though it can move in many different directions, it always comes back home again.

The song below is an old friend. Can you figure out what it is?

Sing it, and then play it. Notice the repeat sign. This makes it twice as long. It is eight measures long. That will give you more time for your own part of the composition.

Here's how to build your rondo: Use the song above as your A section. The A section is about food, so try to continue that theme. Decide on something else you like to eat, then compose a B section. Think of other foods, and then compose a C section.

Look at this example of a B or C section.

Pump - kin pie, pine - ap - ple, plums, plums,

Pump-kin pie, pine - ap - ple plums, plums, Pump-kin pie, pump-kin pie,

plums, plums, plums, plums, pump-kin pie, pine - ap - ple, plums, plums.

Pitches: G A B

Using Recorder Master R•15

Objective

• Students will create and perform a rondo.

Preparation

• Discuss improvisation and composition with students, helping them understand that the basic materials of all composers are the same: tones, rhythmic combinations, instruments or voices, and ideas.

Procedure

• Review the rondo form with students: ABACA.

• Use this simple speech rondo to help students better understand the form.

A — This day is a very happy day.
B — I am going to the circus.
A — This day is a very happy day.
C — There'll be hot dogs and ice cream.
A — This day is a very happy day.

• A simple rhythmic rondo can be established in the same way if students seem to be having difficulty with the concept.

• Guide them through their Recorder Master, setting up groups and helping with ideas for food types.

Name _____ Date _____

Easy Does It

Did you think your right hand would never have to lift a finger— or put one down? Not so! Today you begin with easy E.

Hold up your recorder in the usual way:

- Your left thumb covers the back hole.
- The first three fingers of your left hand cover the top three holes.
- Your right hand lightly supports the recorder.

Now make sure that your right thumb is still supporting the instrument. Use the first two fingers on your right hand to cover the next open holes down. That's all there is to playing the new note E.

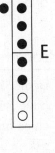

Be careful not to cover the remaining open holes with your other fingers.

You have become good at reading B, A, and G. Now there's another note on a line! Just remember that E is on the bottom line, so it will be easy to keep it straight.

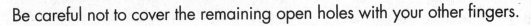

 B    A    G    E

Try these playalongs with the new note—and the old ones, too.

Jamaica Farewell (Chorus)

The Marvelous Toy (Chorus)

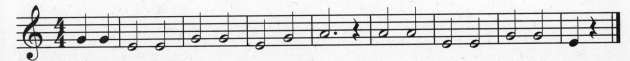

Pitches: E G A

Using Recorder Master R•16

Objective

- Students will learn to play E and use it in two playalongs.

Preparation

- Review finger positions and staff placement of B, A, G.

Procedure

- Demonstrate the fingering for E, and then have students place their recorders on their chins and finger an E. Play the note, and ask students to echo it.

- Have students place their recorders on their chins and finger note patterns you call out, concentrating on back and forth between G and E, but calling other patterns as well.

- Have students draw the notes they know (B, A, and G) along with E on a chalkboard staff.

- Sing pitch names and finger notes on the recorder for the chorus of "Jamaica Farewell" (page 156). Make sure that students hold whole notes for their full value. Then have students play along with the recording, using the playalong on Recorder Master R•16.

- Direct students to read, sing, and finger the playalong for "The Marvelous Toy" (page 182). Have students play the piece just on the recorder and then play along with the recording.

Recorder Master R • 17

And Two to Grow On

The two songs in this lesson are bonus pieces for students who have learned their notes well and who listen to the sound of their recorders as they play them.

The first piece is "An Old Song." Look at the last measure—it's blank. The song does not have an ending. You will have to choose the last note for the song. Choose a note that fits the song and sounds like an ending.

An Old Song

Now try this playalong with "Lukey's Boat." This is a song from Newfoundland.

Lukey's Boat
Descant

Pitches: G A B

Using Recorder Master R•17

Objective

- Students will learn the melody of "An Old Song" and decide what the ending note should be.

- Students will learn a playalong to "Lukey's Boat."

Procedure

- Have students finger both songs before they play them.

- Play "An Old Song" for students. Ask them what is missing (the final note). Play the possible end notes from the notes the students know—B, A, G, and E. Have students choose which note sounds best as the ending. (G is the best choice because it resolves the melody.)

Name _____ Date _____

Moving On with B A G

It's a good thing to make new friends, but it's also important to keep your old friends. In the same way, it's good to learn new notes, but it's also important to remember the old notes. Let's try something new with these old notes.

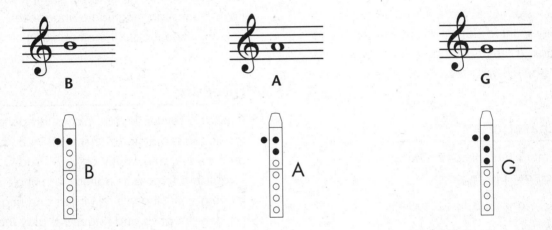

Clap the rhythm pattern below.

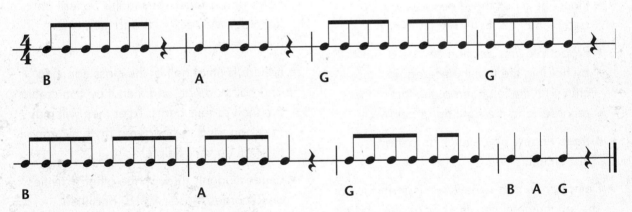

Play the pattern. Half of the class will play it on B, and the other half will play it on G. Then, make a two-part canon. The B players (part 1) start first. The G players (part 2) should start when part 1 begins the second measure.

Now, play the pattern in unison with B, A, and G, according to the pitches written under the notes.

Pitches: B A G

Using Recorder Master R • 18

Objective

- Students will review G, A, and B.

- NOTE TO TEACHER: If students are just now starting to learn the recorder, you may want to start at the beginning of this book. If they have had prior experience, Lesson 18 will serve as a review.

Preparation

- Remind students of the basic rules for recorder playing:

  - Use good posture; sit tall.

  - Breathe gently into the recorder.

  - Tongue with a whispered *doo*.

  - Place the mouthpiece on the lower lip, and then close the upper lip over it.

  - Proper playing position can be achieved by holding the mouthpiece against the chin with the left hand at the top of the recorder and the right hand below.

  - Keep fingers perpendicular to the instrument.

- Demonstrate and review the fingering for B: The left thumb covers the back hole, and the left index finger covers the top hole in front.

- Demonstrate and review fingering for A: With the B fingering in place, cover the next hole with the middle finger.

- Demonstrate and review fingering for G: With the A fingering in place, cover the third hole with the third finger. (If it is hard for students to cover this hole completely, have them slide the middle finger over until they see it from the other side.)

Procedure

- If this is a review lesson, play short patterns for students to echo, at first only on B, then on B and A, and finally on B, A, and G. Establish a three-part pattern for echo-playing with students: (1) listen and finger; (2) sing the pitch and finger; (3) play the pattern.

- Have students identify eighth and quarter notes and quarter rests in the pattern on Recorder Master R•18 and then clap the pattern.

- If there is time, half of the class can clap and half can pat, and then they can create a canon at four beats. Later they will play in canon, and to perform a rhythmic canon first will be very helpful.

- Guide students through the other activities on Recorder Master R•18, and then relate the concepts to pages 14 and 15 in their books.

Name _____ Date _____

Roundabout

Ask yourself about the different ways you can perform a round or canon. Do you have to sing it?

Try making these words into speech canons.

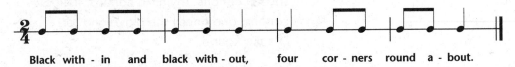

Form two groups. Group 1 begins. Group 2 begins when group 1 begins the second measure.

Try this one next. Perform it as you did the first one. Group 2 should begin when group 1 starts the third measure. Finally, play the rhythm. Group 1 can use rhythm sticks, and group 2 can use hand drums. Think the words while you play the rhythms, but don't speak them out loud.

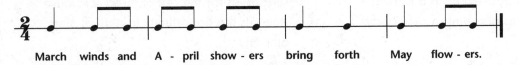

Now try the following rhythmic canon that has no words at all. Clap it in unison. Group 1 should clap it again while group 2 taps or pats it. Do the canon with group 2 starting at the second measure. Then experiment with other starting places for group 2.

After you've done it with rhythms, play the pattern in canon with recorders. Group 1 plays on B, and group 2 plays on G.

Next is a playalong for "Peace Round" in your book. Sing it in unison. Then half of the class can sing it while the other half accompanies on the recorder.

Peace Round
Playalong on B A G

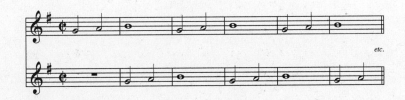

etc.

Pitches: G A B

Using Recorder Master R•19

Objective

- Students will read and perform various forms of canons and will learn a playalong for "Peace Round."

Preparation

- Have students discuss rounds and canons, using examples they are familiar with such as "Three Blind Mice" or "Scotland's Burning."

- Perform the body-percussion canon shown below with students. Students enter after the teacher's first four beats. Note that the teacher always returns to a pat pattern before establishing a new body instrument.

Procedure

- Guide students through activities on Recorder Master, performing and experimenting with speech canons, rhythmic canons, melodic canons, and finally the playalong for "Peace Round."

- Have students experiment with different starting places for group 2 in the rhythmic canon.

- Combine the playalong with the song and with movement activities for the "Peace Canon" on page 16 of the student book. Recorder players stand in place for measures 5 and 6 but can move as suggested for the rest of the piece. Give students the opportunity to play or sing all parts.

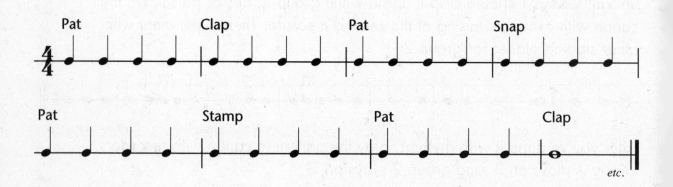

Time for an E Here and There

Your left hand is pretty handy, right? But your right hand has not had much of a chance to play. Today you will change that with E!

• Hold your recorder with G fingering.

• Place the index and middle fingers of your right hand over the next two holes.

• The two fingers should be placed on the two holes at the same time, not one at a time.

• Your right thumb should support the recorder on the back.

Cover the holes completely, and play the following patterns on long notes. Remember to whisper *doo*.

G – E   G – G – E   G – A – G – E   B – E   B – A – G – E

Then go the other way, and play these patterns.

E – G   E – E – G – G   E – B   E – G – A – B – E

Here is a playalong for "Most Done Ling'rin Here"—starring E. "Ling'rin" is another way to spell "lingering." If you don't know what it means, look it up in a dictionary. See whether you think the playalong fits the definition.

**Most Done Ling'rin Here
Playalong**

Pitches: *B A G E*

Objective

• Students will review E on the recorder.

Preparation

• There can never be too much echo play, and it is always an excellent way to start the class. Begin with the notes that students have known the longest—B, A, and G—and then insert E.

Procedure

• Review fingering for E. Show students that, with the left hand positioned for fingering G, the two right-hand fingers should act together in covering the holes, not first the index finger and then the middle finger.

• Challenge students to begin looking away from their finger action—to feel the proper positions rather than looking at them.

• Guide pairs of students in giving echoes to each other, and then combine pairs to play their pieces together.

• Have students practice the playalong for "Most Done Ling'rin Here" (page 65) to gain confidence in adding the E (right hand playing) to notes they are already comfortable with.

• Try an E – B drone on alto xylophone or other melodic percussion with the playalong, first with the recorder alone and then with the song.

You Know the Answer

How many times is the question asked in the chorus of "Oh, Won't You Sit Down?" on page 70 in your book? Does the answer change when the question is repeated? Look at the notes in the repeated answer. Do they move very far from each other?

Half of your class can sing the question while the other half plays the answer. Then you can switch parts.

At last the responder tells why he can't sit down! You will notice that the notes remain the same.

Sing the questions, and play all of the answers. Finally, play the last phrase.

Work with a partner, and make up a melody for another answer. Think of a new way to arrange the notes so that it becomes your answer. Remember that you have a fourth note to work with—E. Try to make your answer last just as long as the answers you've been playing. After you and your partner have created a new answer, join with another pair. Take turns singing the question and playing your new answers.

In the verse of the song, which comes after the chorus, the question will be easy for you to play. You already know the answer. Here is the question.

Make up a different answer to the question asked in the verse. Make it the same length as the answers in the verse.

Pitches: B A G E

Using Recorder Master R•21

Objective

- Students will create responses to the calls in "Oh, Won't You Sit Down?"

Preparation

- Discuss and review question-and-answer activities. Remind students of the "rules" for a good answer: Have the answer in some way related to the question; have the answer be about the same length as the question. Tell students that the "game" of question-and-answer comes from an old form of music called call and response. This form has been used in many ways and by many groups of people, especially in America's past. It often took its form as a work song. In churches it would serve sometimes as a way to let the congregation know the words to their hymns. For students, it is a fun way to improvise or create their music.

Procedure

- Have students practice improvising answers to the teacher's questions. Play a two-measure phrase using notes of the G pentatonic scale, and have students answer, all at the same time, in phrases made up of B, A, G, and E.

- Guide students through the Recorder Master to the final performance of their creative work with the song on page 70.

- When students work with partners, tell them that they can use the same words and rhythm, or they can change the rhythm. Remind them to make answer last just as long as the answers they've been playing.

- As a closing activity, have the partners and larger groups of four play a rotation game.

  - Give each person a number.

  - Number 1 asks the first question.

  - Number 2 improvises the answer.

  - Number 3 asks the next question.

  - Number 4 improvises the answer.

Have students rotate through the roles: number 1 becomes number 2, 2 becomes 3, 3 becomes 4, 4 becomes 1. Then start the question-and-answer. Have students change roles until all four have played each role.

Name _____ Date _____

Bringing D into the Picture

You already know E. Now it is time to add D, the next note in line on the way down the recorder. To play a D, put the first three fingers of your right hand over the three holes down from G. Now you're using all your fingers except your pinkie.

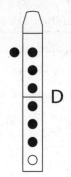

Adding this note is an important step because now you have all five notes of the pentatonic scale in G.

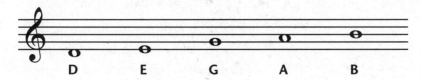

Think back to "Oh, Won't You Sit Down?" Remember the answer to the questions of the chorus *(Lord, I can't sit down)*. Think of the last phrase *('Cause I just got to Heaven, gonna look aroun.")*. Try to play them from memory. All you need is the question *(Oh, won't you sit down?)*, and you'll know the entire chorus.

Review the question and answers for the verse. Now you are able to play the whole song on your recorder!

Now let's check where on the staff you'll find these notes—and give you a chance to write them there. Your teacher will give you staff paper.

G – E   G – E – G – A   E – G – A – D

D – A – B – G – E   B – G – A – B – E – D   D – G – D – A – E

Pitches: D E G A B

Using Recorder Master R•22

Objectives

- Students will learn to play D on the recorder.
- Students will practice writing the notes of the G pentatonic scale in plagel form (D E G A B) on the staff.

Preparation

- Have students echo patterns including E.
- Have students echo answers from "Oh, Won't You Sit Down?"

Procedure

- Demonstrate the fingering for D on the recorder by fingering E and then covering the next hole with the third finger of the right hand. Have students push their fingers across the recorder until the hole is completely covered. Caution students about too forceful a breath while playing this note. Lower notes require less breath.
- Have students echo patterns of E to D, played slowly. Then have them play down the G pentatonic scale.
- Guide students through activities on Recorder Master R•22.

- After students have mastered playing "Oh, Won't You Sit Down?" by memory, have them perform it in a variety of ways.

  - Partners or teammates can take turns with questions and answers.
  - A soloist can play or sing the questions, and the whole class can answer.
  - Students can create their own answers.
  - Students can try other variations of questions and answers, vocally and on the recorder.

- Provide staff paper. Before students begin to write, show on the board the position of D below the staff. Point out how the line goes through a note on a line and how a note in a space sits between two lines. Caution students to be very exact when they write the notes so that line notes are *on* the line and space notes *in* the space. Point out that D is actually below the staff.

- Perform "Oh, Won't You Sit Down?" with students playing the entire melody. Then have them suggest other ways to perform it, including incorporating some of their composed phrases from the previous lesson.

Name _____   Date _____

On the Tip of Your Tongue

In this lesson, you will be working with an exciting rhythm. You will also learn a different way to play the recorder—actually, a difference in tonguing to make the new rhythm easier to play.

Listen to the recording, and pat the beat of "Pat Works on the Railroad." How many equal sounds is the beat divided into? Listen again, pat the beat, and whisper *galloping, galloping, galloping, galloping, galloping, galloping, galloping home.* You will hear three syllables per word and three eighth notes per beat.

When you play this rhythm on your recorder, tongue with a *tuh* whisper instead of the *doo* that you have been using. *Tuh* comes right from the tip of the tongue, very near (but not touching) the teeth.

Limericks are poems that are usually funny. They always have the rhythm of an upbeat and beats divided into threes. Look at this limerick, read it, and clap its beat.

> There was an old man of Peru,
> Who dreamt he was eating his shoe.
> He woke in the night
> In a terrible fright,
> And found it was perfectly true.

Try the playalong on E, G, and B. Play it alone, and then try it as an accompaniment to the limerick. Finally, play it with "Pat Works on the Railroad."

Pat Works on the Railroad

Improvise a tune for the limerick on the G pentatonic notes you know.

Pitches: E G B

Using Recorder Master R • 23

Objective

- Students will perform $\frac{6}{8}$ meter patterns in a playalong with "Pat Works on the Railroad."

Preparation

- Use echo practice to begin the lesson. Use some of the notes and rhythms from "Pat Works on the Railroad."

- Demonstrate the different tonguing to make the eighth notes clearer and cleaner, using *tuh* rather than *doo*. The tongue is near the front teeth, but not touching them. Have students place their recorders on their chins, whispering *tuh tuh tuh tuh*.

Procedure

- Have students share other limericks they might know. Tell students to read them with strong rhythm while clapping or patting the beat.

- Have students explain the characteristics of limericks. If there is time, have students write limericks of their own. Then invite them to set their limericks to music.

- Form three groups—recorder players, singers, and dancers. The groups will perform to "Pat Works on the Railroad." Allow all students to have the opportunity to perform all three roles.

Name _____ Date _____

Speaking of Intervals

A melody is made up of intervals—steps, skips, and leaps. All intervals have names. There is even a name for two notes that stay in the same place: unison. Whether you realize it or not, you have been playing six different kinds of intervals: unisons, seconds, thirds, fourths, fifths, and sixths.

Some intervals sound very good when played together; others do not sound as good. All of the intervals in a pentatonic scale sound good together. Here's what they look like on the staff, first played separately and then together.

When you sing and listen to "Water Come a Me Eye," think about how the melody goes up or down on the words "water come a me eye." The first time, it goes mostly up. The second time, it starts up and then comes back down. Now look at the third and fourth measures of the playalong. In which direction does that melody go? Two melodies going in opposite directions from each other often make very good harmony.

Play the descant playalong. The rhythm is exactly like the words "water come a me eye." Notice the first two measures of the refrain. What interval are you playing there? Play it alone, and then play it while part of the class sings along with the recording.

Water Come a Me Eye

For additional practice, find three seconds, two thirds, two fourths, two fifths, and one sixth in the pentatonic scale.

Pitches: D E G A B

Using Recorder Master R•24

Objectives

- Students will learn that a musical interval is the distance between two notes.

- Students will learn that a melody is composed of a series of intervals.

- Students will learn a playalong descant to "Water Come a Me Eye."

Preparation

- Remind students that intervals pertain to distance. In music, an interval is the distance between two notes.

- Have students experience the intervals of a third, and a fifth. Have half of the class play and hold an E while the other half plays eight quarter notes on G. Then have the first group play and hold an E while the second group plays eight quarter notes on B. Direct students to switch parts and repeat the exercise. (Note to teacher: the interval from E to G is actually a minor third.)

Procedure

- Discuss intervals. Show on the board how intervals are built (both melodic and harmonic) with the tones of the G pentatonic scale. Acknowledge the gaps in the scale, and explain how to name them, counting the lower note as 1 and then counting up the lines and spaces to the upper note. For instance, the notes D to G make the interval of a fourth—D (1), E (2), gap (3), and G (4).

- Show students that a melody is composed of a series of intervals. For instance, point to the notes in "Lord, I Can't Sit Down." Have students sing the pitches. Then point out to them the thirds and second. (You may use an example from any song that students know.)

- Have students clap and speak the phrase, "water come a me eye." Tell students to name the pitches in the third and fourth measures of the playalong. Students should sing and finger the pitches on the recorder and then play them.

- Challenge students to perform the playalong with the recording while half of the class sings.

- Provide students with staff paper, and help them notate the intervals of the G pentatonic scale.

Name _____ Date _____

A Double Dose of D

One D is not enough. It's time to learn high D. Hold your recorder in position for fingering G. Lift your thumb and the first and third fingers. Keep your middle finger in place.

D^I

Practice moving back and forth between G and D^I a few times: $G - D^I \ G - D^I \ G - D^I$.

Are you familiar with an octave, an octagon, or an octopus? *Oct-* is a prefix that means "eight." An octave is an interval that spans eight tones. Its first and last tones have the same name, but one is eight tones higher than the other—D to D, G to G, and all the others.

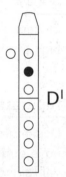

D^I

Practice writing Ds on a staff. Notice that low D is in a space just under the staff, and high D (D^I) is on the fourth line of the staff. When notes have the same name but are an octave apart, one is in a space and one is on a line. If the lower one is in a space, the higher one is on a line, and if the lower one is on a line, the higher one is in a space.

With a partner, play some patterns with your new D.

$D - D^I - D$	$D^I - A - D^I$	$A - D^I - D$
$B - A - D^I$	$D^I - D - A - D$	$A - B - A - D^I$

Play the new D^I in this playalong.

Old Ark's a-Moverin'

Pitches: *D E G A B D^I*

Using Recorder Master R•25

Objectives

- Students will learn to recognize and play high D (D^1).

- Students will learn the meaning of *octave*.

- Students will learn a playalong including high D and an eighth-quarter-eighth rhythm.

Preparation

- Demonstrate silent fingering of patterns, and have students practice them. Then proceed with standard echo practice: listen and finger, sing and finger, play. Include all the notes of the G pentatonic scale that students have learned so far.

Procedure

- Initially, it is difficult for students to control their fingers when playing high D. Demonstrate the fingering between G and high D, and have students practice it silently with you.

- Discuss octaves, reviewing the procedure for counting notes in an interval.

- Invite volunteers to write high and low Ds on a staff on the board. Provide staff paper for the entire class to practice writing them.

- Lead students in clapping the rhythm for the short-long-short pattern in the playalong. Use the words "old ark she rock" in the song on page 130 of the student book.

- Have students look at the notes for the playalong as they listen to the recording of the song. Discuss the places where one part echoes or answers the other.

- Direct students to play the playalong with the recording.

- Encourage students to play the Music Alphabet Word Game. Students make up words from the letters of the music alphabet—A B C D E F G. Students can work individually or in teams to find as many words as they can. Have them write the words in music notation on a staff and then play the words or have other teams play them.

Recorder Master R • 26

High C

It's time to learn high C. Hold your recorder with the fingering for high D, and then put your thumb over the thumb hole in back.

Practice this phrase silently and slowly until you have it memorized: D¹ – C¹ – D¹ – A – G – G – A. Now play it.

Remember that an interval is the distance between two notes. Intervals are the ingredients of a melody. Here is a set of fourths— all of them found in "Bamboo Flute" on page 134 in your book. Some of the intervals appear as they are here, and others go in the opposite direction. How many fourths can you find in the song? Play each fourth in the example below four times.

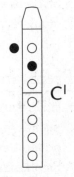

C¹

Now look at the playalong. Count the fourths. Determine if all of the fourths in the example above are found in the playalong. Listen to the recording of "Bamboo Flute" while you watch the notes and tap the beat in the playalong. Be sure to observe the rests. As you listen a second time, finger the notes of the playalong. Now play with the recording.

**Bamboo Flute
Playalong**

Pitches:
E G A C¹ D¹

Using Recorder Master R•26

Objectives

- Students will learn to recognize and play high C (C^1) on the recorder.

- Students will learn a playalong that uses many fourths.

Preparation

- Have students silently practice all of the pitches they know. Then have them echo patterns that you play on these pitches. Emphasize D and A. This will make it easier to play the new note C^1.

- Remind students that A to D is a fourth, and have them count the pitches (and gap) between the two notes.

Procedure

- Demonstrate the fingering for C^1, and have students practice going from C^1 to D^1 several times. Give them rhythm patterns to echo on those notes, and then add A to the echoes.

- Discuss the fourths on the RM, and guide students in finding fourths in "Bamboo Flute" in their books.

- Have them play the 4ths in the exercise.

- Guide them in observing the measures of rests in the playalong.

- When students are able to perform the playalong with the recording, form two groups. Have half of the class sing while the other half performs the playalong on recorder. Give everyone the opportunity to play and sing.

- Point out that the playalong imitates "Bamboo Flute" most of the way through.

Hearing and Playing Chords

Any time you sing a canon or play a part to go with a song, you are making harmony. Harmony is a combination of tones sounded together.

Many songs can be accompanied by three primary chords. The notes in these chords can create a harmony with the melody. Each chord has a number name, written in Roman numerals. The number is the corresponding scale tone. For example, in the key of G major, the I chord starts on G. The IV chord starts on C, the fourth step. The V chord starts on D, the fifth step of the G major scale. If you play those root tones at the right places, you will have a harmonious accompaniment.

Listen to the recording of "This Land Is Your Land," and play the root tones your teacher points to. They will be G, C, or D.

You can make the chords or harmonies richer by adding the other notes found in the chords. Below you will see versions of these chords.

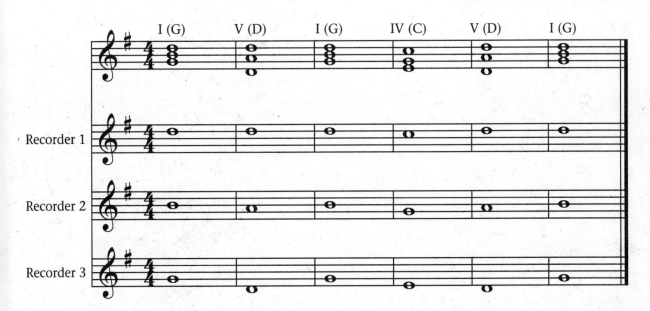

Now play the full chords as your teacher points to the chart. Now play them with the recording. The chords are written for you in your book, with letter names rather than number names.

Pitches: $D\ E\ G\ A\ B\ C^l\ D^l$

Using Recorder Master R•27

Objective

- Students will hear and play the primary chords to accompany "This Land Is Your Land."

Preparation

- Review the meaning of harmony, reminding students of the occasions when they have created harmony.

- Prepare a chart, or use the board, to show I, IV, V, and their corresponding pitch names in G major: G, C, and D. Students will be able to look at this chart and play the appropriate notes of the chords as you point to the chord names.

- Make sure that students are able to play D, D¹, B, A, G, C¹, and E.

Procedure

- Have students play the root tone as you point to chords at random on the chart.

- Have students play the root tones while listening to the recording of "This Land Is Your Land." Point to the proper chord on the chart.

- Have all of the students read each part of the primary chords exercise separately. Discuss any problem they may have with the notes.

- Form three groups, and assign a part to each group. Direct groups to play their part of the chord and listen very carefully to how their note fits in.

- Each group should memorize their notes for the three chords. Have them play the full chords as you indicate while students play with the recording of "This Land Is Your Land."

Cracking the Code

Music written on a page is like a code. To break the code, you have to find the symbols and put them together in a logical way.

You need to analyze the music that you see. Ask yourself these questions about the playalong for "The Old Carrion Crow" at the bottom of the page.

- What is the meter of the piece?
- What kinds of notes are to be played?
- How many parts are being played?
- Are there rests?

- Are there any special tonguing problems?
- What is the proper tempo to play it?
- Why are the two staves joined together?
- Why are the stems of the notes pointed in opposite directions?

In addition, consider looking at the words to the song. They give a clue to the song's mood and the tempo at which it should be played.

Remember, the way to learn a complicated piece is to take it apart, look at its separate parts, and then put it back together for success.

The Old Carrion Crow
Playalong

Pitches:
D E G A B C¹ D¹

Using Recorder Master R•28

Objective

- Students will learn a playalong comprising two accompanying parts and solos.

Preparation

- Prepare two charts, each divided into two sections. The first chart should have the notes A – G – A – A – A in one section and the notes C^I – B – C^I in the other section. The second chart should have the notes D – E – D – E – D in one section and A – G – A in the other.

- Have students read both charts. Form two groups that will play together. One group will play the notes on the first chart, and the other group will play the notes on the second chart.

Procedure

- Call attention to the elements of the score and their meaning:

  - Two staffs joined together
  - Direction of the stems
  - Meter
  - Rests
  - Location of the solos in relation to other parts

- Have students clap the rhythm on the lower staff. Remind them to observe the rests carefully.

- Help students understand or decode the stem direction of the notes on the lower staff. Explain that all of the notes with the stem up are one part and that all of the notes with the stems going down are another part. Have students play the notes with the stems going up. Then have them play the notes with the stems going down. Form two groups, and have one group play the stem-up notes and the other play the stem-down notes. When students have mastered playing the parts together, have them play along with the recording.

- Pat and speak the rhythm for solo part 1: "The crow, the crow, the old carrion crow, fol-the-rid-dle, all the rid-dle, hey ding doh." Clap and speak the rhythm for solo part 2: "Once a tailor shot his cross-bow, once a tailor shot."

- Invite volunteers to play the solos. Have them finger the notes slowly and then sing before playing the parts.

- Combine the solo and accompaniment parts, and have students play with the recording.

Name _____   Date _____

Compose with Poetry

Everything in today's lesson is in triple meter. The best way to understand a meter is to move to it. First, finger these pitches: D¹ – C¹ – A – E. Follow your teacher's instructions to play the pitches and move in rhythm.

Try something a little harder. First clap these patterns, and then play them four times on each pitch as you move to the rhythm.

Play each pattern four times on each pitch: D¹ C¹ A E

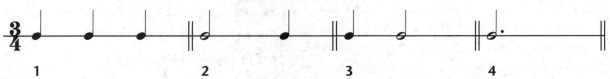

Now you are ready for the playalong. Before you play, analyze it. Look at the meter (3) and the rhythm. Look at the pitches (C¹, D¹, and A). First, play it once without the recording, and then play it with the recording. Notice that there is no playalong for the verse of "Las Mañanitas," only for the chorus.

Las Mañanitas (Chorus)
Playalong

Next, you are going to be a composer. Here are the things you have to work with.

- the meter in 3   • either of the poems below
- the pitches D¹, C¹, A, and E

Here are two poems. Choose the one in English or the one in Spanish.

The Man in the Moon looked out of the moon,   De los caballitos
Looked out of the moon and said,   que vienen y van,
"'Tis time for all students on the earth   el que más me gusta
To think about getting to bed."   Es este alazán.

Your teacher will explain what to do.

Pitches: E A D¹ C¹

Using Recorder Master R•29

Objectives

- Students will learn a playalong for "Las Mañanitas."
- Students will compose music for a poem.

Preparation

- Discuss meter with students, leading them to speak about accents or stressed beats as the way we distinguish meter. Practice clapping a few patterns in twos, fours, and threes.
- Make sure that students are able to play D^l, C^l, A, and E.

Procedure

- Invite students to gently sway left and right as they listen to the recording for "Las mañanitas." Then encourage them to play the patterns indicated at the top of Recorder Master R•29 on E, A, D^l, or C^l. For reading practice, write the numbered patterns on the board, and have students play the rhythms as you point to them in a random order.
- Talk through the playalong for "Los Mañanitas," guiding students to find the meter, rhythm, and pitches. Have them clap the rhythm, play the melody alone, and then play it with the recording. Finally, have students sing the verse and play the chorus along with the recording.

- Discuss with students the method to use in composing music for a poem. First, read both poems aloud in a rhythmic, accented style. Guide students in choosing one of the poems. (Note: The translation for the Spanish poem is "Of two little horses that come and go, the one I like best is this sorrel.")
- Have students work in pairs and follow these guidelines for the activity.
    - Choose one of the poems.
    - Read the chosen poem aloud several times.
    - Pat the beat as you read the poem in rhythm, stressing the accented first beat.
    - Take one line at a time, and experiment with pitches. Find the pattern of pitches that sounds best for the rhythm and words of the poem.
    - Practice the composition, and write it in musical notation.
- Guide students through the process, and then have them share their compositions with the class.

Stretch Your Music Skills

Here are two words that may be new to you: *augment* and *diminish*.
Augment means "to expand or make larger." *Diminish* means "to decrease
or make smaller." In this lesson, you will perform both of those actions on
an old song you probably know. Play it now in its original form.

Go Tell Aunt Rhody

Next, augment the tune. Double all of the note values—a half note becomes
a whole note, a quarter note becomes a half note, and so forth. The first five
measures are done for you. Complete the song. Notate it, and then play it.

Go Tell Aunt Rhody (Augmentation)

Now it's time to do a diminished version of the song. Cut all of the
note values in half—a half note becomes a quarter note, a quarter note
becomes an eighth note, and so forth. Complete the diminished version.
Notate it, and then play it.

Go Tell Aunt Rhody (Diminution)

If you wanted all three versions of "Go Tell Aunt Rhody" to
be played together and end at the same time, how many
times would each version of the song need to be played?

Pitches: G A B D

Using Recorder Master R•30

Objective

- Students will explore augmentation and diminution.

Preparation

- Have students work through the lesson in their books on pages 216 and 217, speaking the poem in augmented form.

Procedure

- Discuss the meanings of the terms *augment* and *diminish*.

- Guide students through the activities of Recorder Master R•30.

- If students are having difficulty keeping the steady beat, play a hand drum as a metronome while they are playing.

- Keep the tempo the same while students clap each of the versions. Have students play all three of them.

- If the augmented version is played through once, the original version will require two repetitions and the diminished version will be played four times.

- Form three groups, and have them tap the beat while playing their parts. Everyone will be tapping the same tempo, but each group will play the entire piece a different number of times.

Changing Tonal Centers

You know that there is a difference in sound between major and minor tonality. In the song "A la nanita nana" you find both major and minor. Look through the song, and you will see that it has two key signatures. However, both key signatures have the same note for the tonal center or home tone.

Listen to the recording, and raise your hand when you hear a change from minor to major or from major to minor. Listen again, and sing the melody.

Analyze the playalong at the bottom of the page. Notice that it is in triple meter. Look at the rhythm patterns below and identify them in the notation.

Listen to the recording again and clap the rhythm.

Did you hear distinct home tones at the end of both sections A and B? You know that the tonal center is D in both sections. Because of their scales, the D tonal center for section A is *la,* and the D tonal center for section B is *do.*

Play the playalong by itself, and then play it with the recording.

A la nanita nana

Pitches: *D E G A B D¹*

Using Recorder Master R•31

Objective

- Students will learn a playalong with both major and minor tonal centers.

Preparation

- Review students' experience with major and minor tonalities. Sing very slowly in pitch syllables a "major/minor" scale beginning on A below middle C: *la ti do re mi fa so la,* and/or play the same scale on the piano. (The students cannot play the D major and D minor scales because they do not know fingerings for F, F#, or B♭.)

Procedure

- Guide students through the activities of the Recorder Master.

- If there are too many different rhythms for students to play easily, organize them into three groups. Assign section A to one group, the first half of section B to the second group, and the second half of section B to the third group.

Name _____   Date _____

A Sharp Lookout

Sometimes a melody needs to go up or down by a half step rather than a whole step. When this is the case, we often make a note sharp or flat. A sharp is a half step higher, and a flat is a half step lower.

The next note you are going to learn is F sharp (F#). When a sharp is placed on the F line in a key signature, it means that all Fs in the piece are played as F#.

With your left hand in position for G, skip the next hole, and place the second and third fingers of your right hand over the next two holes. That is the fingering for F#.

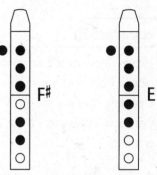

Practice fingering these patterns.

G – F# – G   G – E – G   E – F# – E   G – F# – E   E – F# – G   F# – E – G

Here is the introduction and the ostinato that is played and sung throughout the rest of the piece.

Zum gali gali (ostinato)

Recorder 1, 2

Voices

Zum   ga - li,   ga - li,   ga - li,   zum   ga - li,   ga - li.

Repeat throughout the piece

Now here is the rest of the playalong. Clap the rhythm as you listen to the recording. Notice the next-to-last note—F#. Finger all the notes silently as you listen once again, and then play it with the recording.

Zum gali gali

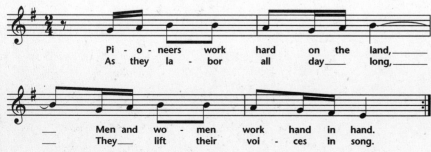

Pi - o - neers   work   hard   on   the   land,____
As   they   la - bor   all   day____   long,____

____   Men and   wo - men   work   hand   in   hand.
____   They____   lift   their   voi - ces   in   song.

Pitches: E F# G A B

Using Recorder Master R•32

Objective

- Students will learn to recognize and play an F♯ on the recorder.

Preparation

- Have students tell what they know about flats and sharps in music notation. Demonstrate on piano, voice, and melodic percussion how a flat or sharp affects a tone.

Procedure

- Demonstrate the fingering for F♯, and have students finger it silently and then play it aloud.

- Call out several patterns that include F♯, especially patterns going to and from G and E. Ask students to finger the patterns silently and then play them aloud.

- Guide students through the activities of Recorder Master R•32.

- Help students analyze the ostinato. Remind them that the stem direction of the notes on the top staff indicates separate parts. Form three groups to practice the ostinato. One group plays the recorder 1 part, one group plays the recorder 2 part, and the third group sings the vocal part. Give students the opportunity to play all three roles.

- In the playalong for "Zum gali gali," students will have to play the G – F♯ – E pattern, so have them practice the pattern several times before trying the playalong.

- Put the ostinato and playalong together. Form four groups, one for each part, and play the entire piece. Have groups switch roles so that everyone has the opportunity to perform each part.

Name _____ Date _____

A Minor Setting

"¿Quién es ese pajarito?" is in a minor tonality and a triple meter.

Listen to the recording, and pat-clap the rhythm. Then finger the playalong as you listen to the recording again.

Perform the playalong without the recording. Some of your classmates can play hand drums quietly to keep the beat, and others can play finger cymbals on every first beat. After you have practiced, play along with the recording.

¿Quién es ese pajarito?
Playalong

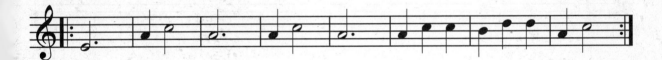

Pitches: E G A B C¹ D¹

Using Recorder Master R•33

Objective

- Students will learn a playalong with "¿Quién es ese pajarito?"

Preparation

- Give students echo phrases in triple meter with an A minor tonality (see below).

Procedure

- Discuss students' perceptions of music in a minor tonality.

- Demonstrate a variety of body percussion patterns in triple meter. Have students create their own body percussion patterns that establish a strong feeling of triple meter.

- Identify the different beat groupings within the playalong: dotted half note, half note–quarter note, three quarter notes, and quarter note–half note.

- Assign some students to play hand drums and finger cymbals. The students playing drums quietly play a three-beat, unaccented pattern. The students playing finger cymbals should play on the downbeat of each measure. Allow the players to play along with the recording, carefully keeping a steady beat.

- Have the entire class perform along with the recording. Add in the parts one by one. Begin with the hand drums, and then add the finger cymbals, the recorders, and finally the singers.

Name _____   Date _____

A Blueprint for Music

If you were going to build a house, you would have to start with a plan—the size of the house, its shape, where it will be placed on the land. You would need to make decisions about the type of materials you would use—lumber, bricks, adobe. If you were the contractor building a house, you would follow the architect's plans, or the blueprint, and you would use materials suggested by the owner.

In this lesson you are to be the music contractor. You will be given the plan and the materials, but you will be able to make your music in the shape you want with the plan and materials you have.

First, analyze this Russian folk song. How many phrases are there? How long is each phrase? What is the key signature? How are the phrases alike and different? What is the tonal center?

Clap the rhythm. Listen to the recording, and finger the song silently on your recorder. Now you are ready to play it.

Beryoza

You are ready to start building. For this song, use D, E, G, A, and B. Review your plan—tonal center E, four 3-measure phrases, and anything else you discovered in your analysis of the piece. Work with a partner. When you have finished, notate your composition on staff paper and share it with the class.

Beryoza
Descant

Pitches:
E F♯ G A B D

Using Recorder Master R•34

Objective

- Students will compose a 12-measure piece with the pitches D, E, G, A, and B.

Preparation

- Review fingering for short phrases including F#. Use these phrases or others: G – F# – G, E – F# – G, E – F# – E.

Procedure

- Guide students in analyzing "Beryoza," using the questions on Recorder Master R•34.

- Have students play "Beryoza" with the recording.

- Guide their composing with the given pitches and form.

- Have them play the descant with "Beryoza."

- Have half of the class play "Beryoza" while the other half plays the descant.

- Invite volunteers to share their compositions with the class.

Two Christmas Songs

"Joy to the World" is a well-known Christmas song. Play this descant with the recording, and then take turns with half of the class singing and half playing the descant.

Joy to the World
Descant

Except for C♯, you know all of the notes in the melody of "Joy to the World." The fingering for C♯ is very easy.

"Entren, santos peregrinos" is an old Christmas song that is sung in Mexico and the United States. It is a part of a special celebration known as "Las Posadas." Like many folk songs in Spanish, the harmony can be sung or played in thirds.

C♯

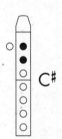

C♯

Entren Santos Peregrinos

Pitches: D E F♯ G A B C♯ D¹

Using Recorder Master R•35

Objective

• Students will learn descants to two Christmas songs.

Procedure

• Demonstrate C# fingering. Have students finger silently patterns such as D – C# – D, D – C# – B, and so on. Challenge them to play the melody of "Joy to the World" by ear.

• Guide them in analyzing the descant to "Joy to the World," especially the measures of rest.

• Have students read and sing pitch names for "Entren, santos peregrinos" in thirds and then play it with the recording.

• Remind students about stem direction indicating the notes in different parts.

All in Good Time

An interesting thing about Switzerland is its languages. It is a landlocked country that touches France, Italy, Germany, and Austria. Because of this, it is a multi-language country. French, Italian, and German are three of Switzerland's official languages. The words for "L'inverno e gia passato" are written in Italian, and they express a happy anticipation of springtime.

In the playalong you have lots of rests between the "cuckoo calls." Be sure to watch and count carefully so that there is a full measure as well as an extra half beat of rest each time before you play.

L'inverno e gia passato
The Winter Is Over
Descant

Pitches: D F♯ G A B C¹ D¹

Using Recorder Master R•36

Objective

- Students will learn a playalong to a Swiss folk song.

Preparation

- Have students tell what they know about Switzerland.

Procedure

- Guide students through a rhythmic analysis of the descant. Reinforce their understanding that rests must be given the full amount of time even though they are not sounded.

- Have half of the students pat the steady beat and the other half clap the rhythm. After students can play the rhythms, have them play it on hand drums and rhythm sticks.

- Have students practice the recorder part, carefully observing the rests.

- Play the recording, and have different groups of students play along on recorder, hand drums, and rhythm sticks.

Index of Songs

Soprano Recorder Fingering Chart

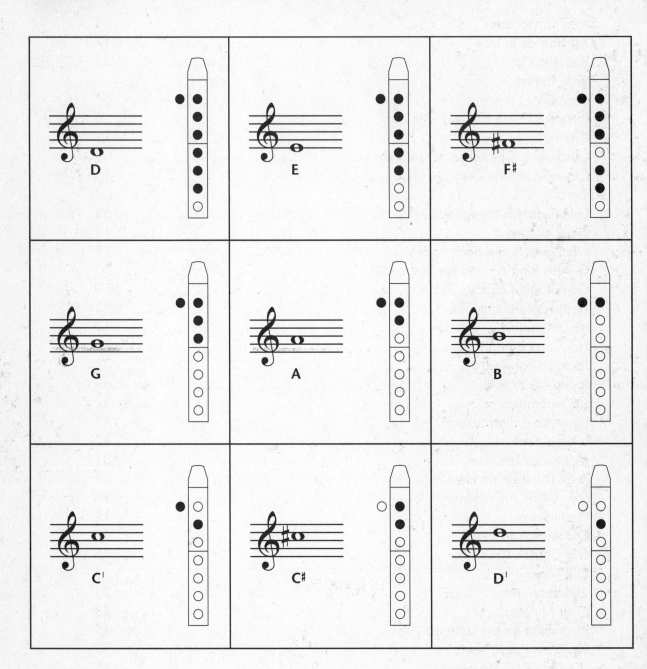